Barbecues

Checkerboard Cookbooks

NEW YORK

Copyright © by Gruppo Editoriale Fabbri, S.p.A., Milan, 1982
Licensee for present English language edition: Bookthrift,
New York, NY, 1982

Adapted from *Griglia, Spiedo, Barbecue*, by Giorgio Mistretta, in the
series "Jolly della Buona Cucina" (Series Editor, Luigi Carnacina;
Photographs by Mario Matteucci, Sandro Pagani, and Romano
Vada)

First published in USA 1982 by Checkerboard Cookbooks
Checkerboard Cookbooks is a trademark of Simon & Schuster, Inc.
Distributed by Bookthrift, New York, NY

Editorial adaptation and production by
Accolade Books, Inc., New York, NY

Editorial director: John Kremitske
Editorial consultant: Nancy Parilla Macagno
Recipe editing and adaptation: Pam Rabin, Dale McAdoo
Introduction by: Stephen Schmidt
Layout: Marcia Rizzi
Cover design: Michael Simon

ALL RIGHTS RESERVED

ISBN 0-89673-119-7

Printed in Italy

Introduction

Barbecue—Ancient Way of Cooking, Popular Modern Pastime

BARBECUING

The word *barbecue*, or *barbeque*, comes from French; but early on it became naturalized as an American expression. In a strict sense, it means cooking in the open air and is a corruption of the French expression *de la barbe à la queue* (literally, "from the beard to the tail"), implying that the animal is cooked whole, skewered on a long spit from head to tail, sometimes directly in or over a large pit lined with glowing coals.

In all true barbecuing, the food is subjected to the heat, but *not* the flame itself, from a wood or charcoal fire (unless, of course, modern equipment requiring other fuels is used). When planning a barbecue, you should first choose the type and quantity of fuel and gauge the heat intensity and timing according to the kind of food to be cooked.

In barbecuing nowadays, an entire animal is seldom roasted whole, but equipment for use in cooking over charcoal is generally referred to as "barbecuing" equipment even if it is capable of accommodating nothing larger than a pair of club steaks. From a practical viewpoint, such simple and scaled-down equipment is ordinarily adequate to grill food in the open air—even if on the balcony or terrace of a city apartment. For that matter, with its growth in popularity and specialized apparatus, barbecuing need not be done exclusively outdoors. But the aromas of food cooking over an open fire, and the hearty appetites they encourage, remain irresistible and highly enjoyable.

We precede our detailed discussion of the various methods of barbecuing and their rules for best results with a revealing quote from the Frenchman Auguste Escoffier, one of the great masters of modern gastronomy. In his celebrated *Guide culinaire*, he wrote: "The entire theory of this kind of cooking can be summed up in a few words: Regulate the intensity of the heat to suit the cut of meat to be cooked—its size, quality, and even the degree to which it is perishable, in the case of liver, kidney, and so forth. But only experience can serve as a sure guide. Theory, however detailed, can only show the way, lay down a few basic rules. It can never substitute for the eye of a good cook and that ability which is the fruit of long practice." In a word, then, this is one cooking technique where practice does indeed make perfect—or at least better!

COOKING ON A SPIT

Of the many possible ways of preparing meats, cooking on a spit provides not only one of the most delicious taste treats but also a very healthful one. When meat and other foods are subjected to heat in this manner, a delicate crust gradually forms on the surface, a kind of protective film that traps the savory juices inside, protects nutritional value, and helps retain flavor.

Using a spit offers further advantages. The fat within the meat itself, and that used for basting, melt with exposure to heat and flow downward, thus being largely eliminated. For many dishes, these cooking fats are collected in a drip pan to be used for continued basting, for making sauces and gravies, or for flavoring thick slices of home-style bread or cornmeal patties seved as accompaniments. It is a desirable and healthy characteristic of spit cookery that excess fat is lost, so that a roast or steak arrives at the table appetizingly juicy yet comparatively lean.

For smaller cuts of meat such as steaks, chops, and sausages, a simple grill will generally suffice; but the larger cuts of meat and whole birds are best grilled on a spit. When skewered and cooked on a spit, meat absorbs and cooks with heat radiated directly from the charcoal or wood embers, yet does not come in direct contact with the heat source itself or a hot surface. For large pieces of meat, the distance between the spit and the heat source can be adjusted, and since the spit is continually turning, the food cooks uniformly—a highly desirable feature in any kind of cooking.

It is essential for best results that searing of meat over an open fire (i.e., formation of the protective crust) is uniform. If a fowl or a small roast were exposed to heat action for 10 minutes on one side and only 5 minutes on the other, the result would be noticeably uneven cooking, with part of the meat charred or overcooked while the rest was underdone. Because an automatic spit turns at a constant speed, it ensures uniform and thorough cooking of food in its entirety.

A final important aspect of cooking on the spit is *balancing* the meat: that is, securely fastening it to the spit in properly balanced fashion. Since the meat must not lose its juices during cooking, it should have as few external punctures as possible. Therefore it is advisable to insert the skewer or spit with a single, decisive thrust. The roast or fowl should be well tied and trussed, then have the spit thrust through its heaviest portion to achieve balance.

Fowl and small game should be skewered from back to front, through their cavity. Cuts of meat containing large bones should be skewered diagonally to ensure good balance. Finally, the holding forks attached to most serviceable spits should be fastened securely to keep the meat firmly in position. If carefully skewered, meat will cook on a spit with a minimum loss of tasty and nutritious juices.

GRILLING

Whereas the great advantage of a spit is that it can be set in front of the fire or to one side, higher or lower, according to the requirements of a particular food or recipe, a grill must always be placed above the heat source. The meat itself (or other grilled food) should never be touched by the flame, because such direct contact would result in undesirable burning and production of harmful combustion by-products. Therefore the grill must be set at the proper distance above the heat source to ensure the right temperature. When fastened on the spit, food is cooked with no external contact whatsoever with other substances (except for the spit or skewers themselves). On the grill, however, it must remain in contact with the metal of the grill itself, which rises in temperature as cooking proceeds. Since such contact eventually burns the meat, and unevenly, all cuts should stay on the grill as brief a time as possible for satisfactory cooking.

In cooking on a spit, the cooking juices drip mostly into a drip pan; but in cooking over a grill, they fall directly onto the fire, igniting and causing smoke and possibly unpleasant odors or an unwanted (or excessive) smoky taste. That is why, when you grill, you must watch the cooking constantly and very carefully, in order to shift the food away from any flare-ups caused by drippings. A drip pan should always be used when substantial basting is involved. Although these recommendations may seem too demanding to some outdoor cooks, they should be followed as closely as possible to achieve the best nutritional and taste results. Although grilling is basically a fairly simple way of cooking, it does require very close attention and, preferably, some prior practical experience with or direct observation of the procedure.

The grill must always be kept clean and should be thoroughly preheated before you set food on it for cooking. Whatever food is being cooked—with the exception of the more delicate fish or vegetables—should generally be turned often to guarantee uniform cooking on both sides. When turning food on a grill, do not use a fork, even a so-called "barbecue" or carving fork; the tines will puncture the flesh or pulp and cause desirable sealed-in juices to escape, perhaps even breaking the food apart unappetizingly. Long-handled tongs are the best utensil for this purpose, or else a spatula or even a broad-bladed knife. Nor should a fork be used to test for degree of doneness; instead, test by pressing gently on the meat with the back of a spoon. When properly cooked, the meat should have a resilient feel, resisting the pressure of the spoon. (For perfect medium-rare meat, watch carefully for the moment at which small reddish-pink drops begin appearing on the surface, then remove the meat from the heat immediately.)

PIT BARBECUING

We have left for last an indigenous way of cooking that is at least as ancient as use of a spit or grill—and probably much older. This more difficult method, known as pit barbecuing, is less easy to control, but it is the one approach that provides the hearty and wholesome pleasures of a traditional clambake, pig or wild boar roast, or the splendid Hawaiian luau.

Some experts believe that early American colonists first learned the technique from the native Indians, who used it to cook whole wild game such as deer and buffalo. This is a likely origin, at least so far as the North American system is concerned. Similar practice existed among native groups in Latin America, later adopted most notably by the colorful gauchos of Argentina. But just as cooking on a spit or grill started independently in diverse lands around the world, so pit cooking must have evolved naturally among many peoples without outside influences. If not, how then does one explain the age-old tradition among Sardinian shepherds of cooking wild hare, lamb, and goat in this way, or similarly ancient culinary customs found in Greece, Iberia, and various other regions along the Mediterranean shores, including parts of North Africa and the Middle East?

Just as they learned how to attach pieces of meat to sticks, to roast them over hot coals or embers, ancient cooks eventually discovered the opportunities of cooking an animal carcass in a hole dug in the earth to shield the fire from the wind. The open or partially sealed pit was a remote predecessor of the enclosed oven as a mode of cooking.

There are several known ways of pit cooking. Some dig a hole to fit the size of the animal quite snugly, lay down and burn a fire until the glowing coals are ready, then set in a layer of green or slightly dampened leaves as a bed for the roast and put a leaf cover on top as well (or at clambakes on sandy beaches, a layer of moist seaweed). Another method is to put the carcass in the pit first, cover it with leaves, and build a fire on top or else scatter over the pit hot coals taken from a fire made nearby. Yet a third system, and perhaps best of all, is closer to the working principle of the oven. A pit is dug and lined with flat rocks; the carcass is placed right on the rocks and covered with a layer of leaves and more rocks. A bonfire is built on top and, when reduced to glowing coals, is scattered over the topmost rocks and later scraped away after cooking is complete. Whichever of these rudimentary folk methods is used, the meat is first seasoned with salt, pepper, and herbs or berries picked on the spot.

SOME RULES FROM A MASTER CHEF

The celebrated cooking expert, Brillat-Savarin, author of *La Physiologie du gout*, once wrote: "Roasting cooks are born, not made." Although we don't want to leave it in such discouraging terms, it is true that accomplished roasting cooks reach those heights only by developing fine-tuned observation, along with strong dedication to learning everything about a way of cooking that, at its best, is indeed a fine art. Some basic general rules laid down by Brillat-Savarin are as follows:

1. All red meats, which are rich in juices, should be seared very rapidly; that means, depending on the size of cut, being subjected to a fire hot enough to allow sufficient penetration of heat but, at the same time, with almost no flame.

2. For white meats, the heat intensity must be more evenly regulated so that searing and thorough cooking take place simultaneously.

3. For small game birds, the best source of heat is a wood fire. In this case, the fire must be regulated so there is more flame than concentrated heat.

TIPS FROM THE EXPERTS

Cooking: The food timing table accompanying this Introduction may be enough to help a beginner on his or her way, but many other points should be kept in mind when barbecuing with any of the various common methods. To begin with, the meat must be as dry as possible when placed on the grill. When it has been marinated, as is called for in many recipes, care should be taken to dry it well before cooking it. The marinade, usually made with oil or melted butter, vinegar or lemon juice (or wine), drippings, and herbs and other seasonings, is then used for basting during the actual cooking.

As soon as the meat comes in contact with the hot grill or is exposed to the heat on an open spit or in a rotisserie, it will start forming a thin crust of cooked meat on its surface. Do not begin basting until this crust is formed. Remember that the purpose of basting is to keep the meat surface moist and tender, but only after this protective crust has formed to seal in the juices. Also keep in mind that excessive basting, especially with highly flavored marinades, can instead toughen the meat during prolonged cooking. Be careful to avoid dripping oily marinades onto the glowing coals and causing flare-ups. Careful use of a drip pan and a long-handled pastry brush for basting will prevent such unwanted flare-ups and will conserve flavorful drippings for added use in sauces, gravies, etc.

Seasoning with salt and pepper should be done nearly at the last moment—ideally, after the meat has been taken off the grill. If salt is used too early in cooking, it tends to soften and open up the meat surface, thereby undoing the value of searing and sealing in the nutritious, tasty natural juices.

When the meat is done to taste, don't be in a hurry to carve it. To avoid losing sealed-in juices, unless otherwise specified in the recipe it is best to let the meat stand for 5 to 10 minutes in a warm place while the juices "set" or are distributed throughout its tissues. To carve grilled or roasted meats properly, you should use a special carving board with a groove for catching the juices that run out when it is cut. These can either be poured over the carved meat *au naturel* or be combined with pan drippings to make seasoned gravy or sauces.

The fire: When using a charcoal grill, burn the briquets until you have glowing coals. (The same general rule applies when cooking with a wood fire.) Since the proper fire is so important to the cooking process, one should bear in mind the following factors:

First, the total area of glowing coals should be at least twice as large as that occupied by the food being cooked. (Two or three dozen charcoal briquets are enough for most ordinary barbecuing.) Second, coals should be spread in such a way that their depth near the edges is slightly greater than in the center; this sloping distribution causes the heat to rise and envelop the food being cooked, with little heat being lost. A third rule is never to rake the fire while food is already on the grill, since the resulting change in temperature, even if brief, will have adverse effects on the meat. Once the food has begun to cook, the temperature should remain as uniform as possible. Even if you think the fire is not at its best, leave it as is; disruption of the cooking process and damage to the food will be less than if you try blowing on the fire or raking the coals with a poker.

(Some outdoor gas grills now on the market are an exception to this rule about disturbing the fire once cooking is under way. Fired either by liquid gas sold in tanks or with natural gas fed by a hookup into the regular kitchen supply, this type of burner maintains reliable constant heat that can be precisely adjusted during cooking with no adverse effects on the food.)

USE OF FATS IN BARBECUING

In barbecuing very little use should be made of fats. The way of cooking in itself is one of the most healthful precisely because it lets melted fats run off, to the great enhancement of both flavor and digestibility. Even so, certain meats dry up when exposed to heat if they are not basted with moderate amounts of fat. Some meats even turn leathery and become practically inedible. For these meats, at least some fat must be used, but it should be kept to a minimum. Here are a few general rules about fats that the cook should keep in mind.

Marinating: This is the simplest way to tenderize and flavor meats before cooking. Almost all meats take well to marinating, but the process is ideally suited to lean steaks and fish. An excellent all-purpose marinade is simply oil (preferably olive oil, for flavor) mixed with a little lemon juice and finely chopped parsley. Most meats should be left to marinate for about 1 hour, with frequent turning to ensure adequate flavoring on all sides. After marinating, the meat should be dried thoroughly with a paper towel. During cooking, meats should be basted as often as necessary. A long-handled brush, of the sort used in baking pastry, is well suited for basting meats and other grills.

Larding: This operation serves to introduce slivers of fat in a piece of meat or a whole animal carcass. It is most conveniently done with a larding needle, which can be bought in specialized kitchenware stores. The fat should be cut in long, thin strips. A strip is inserted in the hollow ˙of the needle; the needle is run through the meat and then withdrawn, leaving the larding fat behind. The fat is trimmed so that it does not protrude from the holes made by the needle. Larding is a process that is particularly useful in working with large cuts of very lean meat or whole carcasses.

Barding: This system is used particularly for lean fowl, especially game birds. The animals are wrapped in broad, thin strips of bacon or else thin layers of "barding fat," and the fat is held in place by small metal pins, toothpicks, or even trussing twine. Such preparation must be done before putting a cut of meat or the carcass on the skewer or spit. Usually this fat is removed shortly before the cooking is completed in order to give the meat surface a better chance to brown and become crisp.

Seasoned Butters: In some cases, especially when dealing with red meats, it is better to tenderize the meat not by marinating in oil but by greasing it with some animal fat such as butter or lard. For tenderizing, basting with melted butter is useful; for flavoring, garnish the meat with a pat of seasoned butter just before serving.

GRILLING FISH

Whole fish and firm-fleshed fish steaks can be barbecued directly on the grill, with or without a layer of aluminum foil. Small varieties such as fresh sardines, smelts, and brook trout and delicate fillets are best cooked in a flat, hinged wire grill basket found in stores where barbecue equipment is sold. Different-gauge wire meshes are available, to be chosen according to the type and size of fish—or also small meats—you intend to grill. Shellfish (oysters, clams, mussels, scallops, shrimp, small lobster tails or crayfish) and such delicate-fleshed fish as flounder, sole, and freshwater trout are particularly recommended for grilling in the wire basket. This long-handled device allows you to turn the more delicate fish easily without breaking them apart once the cooking has begun. (It can also save you quite a few burned fingers.)

Fish should always be brushed with oil or melted butter before being placed on the grill and should be basted often during the cooking period to keep from drying out and charring unappetizingly. Once set on the grill, fish should be watched very carefully because it requires a comparatively brief cooking time (see food timing table). A matter of just an extra minute or two can mean the difference between a juicy, tender grilled fish or a dried-out, toughened, inedible one. This is perhaps the area of barbecuing requiring the most diligent care and attention, and the one that will profit most from broad experience at doing it, particularly in saving those often expensive aquatic treats and making them into a truly delicious meal.

BASIC BARBECUING EQUIPMENT

For the novice outdoor cook, it is best to start small and gradually work your way up-scale when it comes to buying barbecue equipment. Some good starters are a lightweight portable unit of the *open brazier* type, even the folding kind, or one of the many modest versions of the *hibachi* type. After some trial and error with such unpretentious apparatus, you can decide how seriously you want to go at barbecuing and invest in more suitably elaborate equipment—or perhaps remain a once-in-a-while backyard cook and stick with your modest grill.

Grills come in all sorts of styles, sizes and prices. The more ambitious—and expensive—models feature such extra conveniences as motor-driven spits, built-in drip pans, utensil racks and storage space, carving boards, air dampers and hoods, and provisions for smoke exhaust. Among the more expensive kinds available are *kettle* (hemispherical) and *wagon* (rectangular) grills; *smoke ovens*, or "smokers" (slow cooking for smoky flavoring); and automatic *electric* and *gas* grills, using radiant heat as their working principle. Some of the selling points of these higher-priced models include their ease of start-up and better possibilities of heat regulation. These grills are frequently available in both permanently installed and portable types.

In choosing among grills, the gratings themselves are an important consideration. Avoid those lighter ones made only of wire; buy grates made of good solid wrought iron or of steel-coated iron. These are preferable both for durability and for ease of cleaning.

Whatever model you select, it is most important to read the manufacturer's instructions carefully and beforehand. This will save you much time and anguish in getting the fire started and bringing it to the proper point for cooking, as well as in the barbecuing process itself and the cleanup afterward. It is essential

to know such basic facts, for instance, as whether or not the firebox needs some foundation or lining (e.g., foil, sand), as a bed for a charcoal or wood fire, and what fuel is best suited to a particular model of grill.

An important caveat here: *Never* use kerosene or gasoline to start your charcoal fire. Kerosene will give an unpleasant odor and taste to the food, and gasoline is much too dangerous to use for such purposes. Also, *never* pour any liquid fire starter on hot coals, even though they seem to have gone out.

There is a good practical rule of thumb for testing a fire for proper cooking temperature: With your hand, palm down, just above the hot coals at the level where the food will cook, begin slowly counting—"one-thousand-one, one-thousand-two, etc." If the heat forces you to pull away your hand at the count of two (roughly, 2 seconds), the coals are a *hot* fire; three, *medium-hot*; four, *medium*; and five or six, *slow* (mainly for warming, not sufficient for cooking).

After each use, your grill should be thoroughly cleaned and then covered. Certain recently developed spray coating products will give the grill an anti-sticking film beforehand that will greatly ease cleaning it afterward. In general, it's easier to clean the grates as soon as possible after barbecuing. This can be done by soaking the grate in a sinkful of hot, soapy water and later rinsing and wiping it clean with a damp cloth. If you don't want to do the cleanup immediately, it helps to wrap the soiled grate in wet paper toweling or newspapers until you're ready to wash it; this keeps the soiled

materials softer for eventual cleaning. For a very greasy, thickly coated grate, you can scour with baking soda sprinkled on a barely damp sponge and then rinse in baking soda and clean water. Stubborn burned-on grease and particles can also be cleaned with soapy scouring pads or a stiff metal brush and scouring powder.

RECOMMENDED BARBECUE ACCESSORIES

These are some of the basic utensils and other accessories most useful to have on hand when barbecuing:

Long-handled pastry brush for basting
Long-handled spatula
Long-handled fork
Long-handled tongs (2 pairs—1 for food, 1 for coals)
Carving knife
Long, thick asbestos oven mitts
Skewers (metal and wooden, depending on use or preference; preferably with handles)
Meat thermometer
Drip pan (for easier cleanup, the disposable aluminum kind)
Hinged wire grill baskets (with various-sized meshes)
Aluminum foil (heavy-duty)
Pliers (for positioning roasts on the spit and tightening the grips, or holding forks)
Metal brush for cleaning grates

FOOD TIMING TABLE FOR GRILLS AND BARBECUES

Type of Food	Thickness (inches)	Type of Fire	Cooking Time (minutes)		
			Rare	Medium	Well-done
Beef					
steak	1	hot	8-10	10-12	15-20
steak with bone	1½	hot	10-12	12-15	15-20
filet mignon	1½	hot	10-12	12-15	15-20
hamburgers	1½	med.-hot	8-10	10-12	12-15
kabob	—	med.-hot	8-10	10-12	12-15
Veal					
scallopini	¼	med.-hot		5-8	10-12
cutlet	½	med.-hot		10-12	12-15
kabob	—	med.-hot		10-12	12-15
large cuts, roasts	—	med.-hot		20/lb	
Pork					
loin chops	¾	medium			15-20
cutlet	½	medium			15-20
large cuts, roasts	—	medium			15-20/lb
kabob	—	medium		10-12	12-15
ham steaks	½	med.-hot		10-15	
Lamb					
rib chops	1	medium		20-25	25-30
shoulder chops	1	medium		25-30	30-35
cutlet	½	medium		8-10	12-15
kabob	—	medium		8-10	12-15
leg	—	medium		12-15/lb	15-20/lb
Fowl					
whole chicken, spitted	—	med.-hot			30-35/lb
chicken, cut in parts	—	med.-hot		20-25	25-30
Cornish hen, squab	—	med.-hot			40-45/lb
small game birds	—	hot		10-15	15-20
Fish					
whole, medium-size	1½	med.-hot		20-25	
whole, small	¾	med.-hot		15-20	
fillets	½	medium		10-12	
slices, steaks	¾	medium		12-15	
shrimp (jumbo)	—	med.-hot		15-20	

Note: The above time indications may serve as a basic guide, but remember that such cooking times are greatly influenced not only by the quality of the meat or other foods used and by the type of fire or equipment but also by such natural factors as altitude, temperature, and wind conditions.

Barbecue Equipment and Accessories

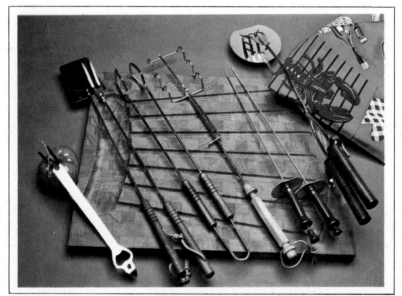

Barbecuing accessories: Long-handled forks, spatulas, and tongs, skewers, a grooved carving board.

◁

▷

Modest-sized portable barbecues for use on a terrace or patio: left to right, square grill with a smoke duct; kettle grill with a spit and grate adjustable according to wind direction; simple tripod grill with a height-adjustable grate.

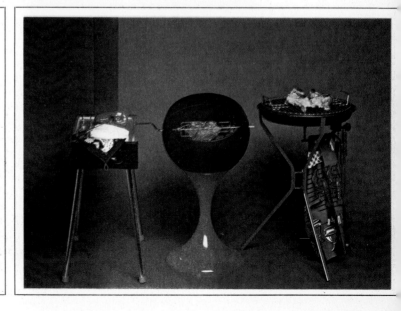

Although open-air barbecuing is regarded as the most natural cooking tradition in its origin, today's manufacturers have designed a wide variety of grills and other apparatus to help even a novice cook prepare tasty barbecued meats, fish, and poultry. Specialized barbecue supply stores now offer a huge selection of charcoal, electric and gas grills, both portable and permanently installed, either with or without all sorts of accessories—tripods, automatic spits, wheels, hoods and chimneys, temperature controls, etc. Shown here is but a small selection of basic equipment from the enormous array available.

△

An assortment of grills that are adaptations of the traditional Japanese type, the *hibachi*.

▷

Left, an electric oven rotisserie with automatic spit; right, an electric covered grill.

Herbs for Barbecuing

The simple natural open-fire cooking done most frequently calls for a special use of herb seasonings, a skill that comes from thorough familiarity with their qualities and from continued practice. Some of the barbecue flavor comes from the fire itself, but nature has made available to the outdoor cook a bountiful supply of herbs that can add variety and distinctive accents to the finished dish.

Besides the herbs you intend to use for cooking on the grill, it is a good idea to have a generous, varied supply of herbs set out in little labeled dishes or cups, for your guests to choose from as individual garnishes in serving themselves. Subtle use of the right herbs in combination with the right foods is the secret of delicious marinades; various chopped fresh herbs can be sprinkled on grilled meats or used in stuffing the cavities of whole fish and poultry. Also, sprigs of fresh rosemary and thyme can be used as flavorful basting brushes. If fresh herbs are not readily available, you can substitute dried herbs, using about one-third the quantity indicated for fresh ones. Below is a list of some herbs commonly used in barbecuing.

Basil:
This is one of the basic herbs in all French and Italian cooking. A sprinkling of fresh basil leaves, not chopped but merely torn in little pieces, can be used to flavor cooked meats just before serving. Minced very fine, basil is an excellent accent for nearly all meats and fish.

Chives:
Finely chopped chives can be sprinkled on grilled steaks; it is also an excellent flavoring for seasoned butters.

Fennel:
The leaves and stalks of fennel are widely used in cooking. It is particularly suited to grilled fish, both for stuffing and for making a bed atop aluminum foil on the grill, on which the fish is then laid for cooking; this slows down the cooking process a bit and gives a marvelous aromatic flavor to the fish. Fennel seeds are also a useful, flavorful ingredient in many grill recipes, such as for sausages and stuffings.

Garlic:
A homely familiar favorite, garlic, used sparingly and subtly, adds irresistible aroma and flavor to a wide range of foods. It is especially fine with pork dishes, steaks, and some poultry recipes. You yourself are probably best aware of how much to use and with what foods you relish it, for reactions to its qualities are highly personal. Needless to say, comparisons between the genuine fresh article and any prepared garlic salts or powders reveal the shortcomings of the latter commercial items.

Marjoram:
This relative of oregano closely resembles it, and can be used either fresh or dried to season almost any sort of meat or fish.

Mint:
Finely chopped mint can be sprinkled on a variety of meats as a distinctive, fresh-tasting garnish after cooking.

Oregano:
A versatile herb, oregano is very useful in open-air cookery, both in marinades and sprinkled on cuts of meat before cooking. It is highly recommended for use in grilling eel and other oily, strong-flavored fish.

Rosemary:

One of the most familiar of all herbs, known from very ancient times, rosemary is often broken in bits and inserted in poultry, lamb, mutton, and pork before cooking. Its subtle, delicious flavor is useful for offsetting any gaminess that may be found in strong-flavored meats such as lamb or mutton.

Sage:

Called for in many recipes, not only in barbecuing but in preparing oven roasts, stews, and other dishes, sage is often used in marinades and for stuffing the cavity of whole fish and poultry before cooking. Fresh sage is especially recommended for all pork dishes, from chops to loin roasts.

Scallions and Shallots:

Chopped very fine, scallions and shallots can be used for flavoring just about any cut of meat or can be mixed with ground beef for hamburgers or various stuffings.

Tarragon:

Chopped tarragon can be sprinkled on meats just before serving and is also recommended for stuffing the cavities of whole fish or poultry before cooking.

Thyme:

Thyme is an indispensable ingredient in preparing marinades for and in cooking lamb and mutton. Either freshly chopped or as a crumbled dried herb, it is also very good with such lighter meats as veal, poultry, and rabbit.

Barbecue Sauces and Seasoned Butters

Béarnaise Sauce

Yield: 4 or more servings

2 sprigs chervil, minced (or generous pinch of
   dried)
2 sprigs tarragon, minced (or pinch of dried)
2 shallots, minced (or scallions)
pepper, freshly ground
5 Tb dry white wine
5 Tb vinegar
3 egg yolks
¾ cup butter
salt

In a saucepan, combine chervil, tarragon (reserving a pinch each for garnish), shallots, a generous pinch of pepper, wine, and vinegar. Simmer until liquid has been reduced by two-thirds. Remove from heat, and cool to lukewarm. Beat egg yolks until thick. Add 1 tablespoon of hot water, and beat for a minute or so longer. Return sauce to low heat, and add egg yolks, beating constantly with a wire whisk. Add butter in small pieces, still whisking constantly. Season to taste with salt, and continue whisking until sauce thickens.

Strain sauce through cheesecloth or a fine sieve, and serve in a sauceboat, sprinkled with reserved minced chervil and tarragon. (Béarnaise Sauce should never be exposed to high heat and should be served at room temperature.)

Curry Sauce

Yield: 4 or more servings

¼ cup minced onion
2 Tb butter
1 Tb chopped parsley
1 small stalk celery, chopped
pinch of thyme
½ bay leaf
nutmeg, freshly grated
4 Tb all-purpose flour
1 tsp curry powder
2 cups chicken or vegetable broth
⅓ cup heavy cream
lemon juice

Sauté onion in butter until wilted. Add chopped parsley and celery, together with thyme, bay leaf, and a pinch of nutmeg. Sprinkle with flour and curry powder, then whisk until well blended. Cook until the mixture begins to brown, then very gradually stir in broth. Bring to a boil, reduce heat, and simmer for about 30 minutes.

Strain the sauce, pressing the solid residue through a sieve, and return to the pan. Bring to a simmer again, stir in heavy cream, and add lemon juice to taste.

Béarnaise Sauce (p. 18)

French Sauce

Yield: 4 or more servings

3–4 scallions, chopped (without green tops)
black peppercorns, crushed
2 Tb dry white wine
2 Tb wine vinegar
3 egg yolks
salt
4 Tb butter, softened
3 Tb tomato purée

In a saucepan, combine chopped scallions, several crushed peppercorns, wine, and vinegar. Over high heat, reduce liquid slightly. Remove sauce from heat, let stand briefly to cool, and beat in egg yolks, lightly beaten together with 1 tablespoon of water. Set over moderate heat again, add salt to taste, then pieces of butter a little at a time, and whisk well until sauce begins thickening. To keep sauce from curdling, make sure it does not boil. Reduce heat to simmer, add tomato purée and, after a minute or two, remove from heat. (Finished sauce should be the consistency of a slightly runny mayonnaise.)

Marot Sauce

Yield: 4 or more servings

¾ lb shelled fresh fava beans (or limas)
2 garlic cloves
2 Tb chopped mint leaves
1 cup grated Parmesan cheese
1 cup grated Romano cheese
about ¾ cup olive oil

Crush fava beans, garlic, and mint leaves in a mortar, or purée in a food processor. Add cheeses and mix well. Very gradually, add enough oil to dilute to the consistency of a fairly thick purée.

Mustard Aioli Sauce

Yield: 4 or more servings

2 egg yolks, lightly beaten
3–4 garlic cloves, chopped
2 Tb lemon juice (or wine vinegar)
1 tsp Dijon mustard
½ tsp salt
black pepper, freshly ground
1 Tb crushed mixed herbs, preferably fresh (e.g.,
*   rosemary, marjoram, thyme; or 1 tsp dried)*
2 Tb chopped parsley
1 cup olive oil

In a blender, combine egg yolks, garlic, lemon juice, mustard, salt, fresh ground pepper, mixed herbs, and parsley. Blend thoroughly on high speed until smooth. Uncover blender, and add oil slowly but in a steady stream while blending on low speed. When sauce becomes so thick that more oil is hard to blend in, add 1 or 2 tablespoons of cold water, and then the remaining oil. Consistency of sauce should be like a light mayonnaise.

Mustard Sauce

Yield: 4 or more servings

⅓ cup Dijon mustard
½ cup oil (preferably olive or sesame)
2 Tb wine vinegar
1 tsp dry white wine (optional)
salt and pepper
pinch of sugar

Combine all ingredients—including salt, pepper, and sugar to taste—in a blender or food processor, and then blend thoroughly. (Blending can also be done by hand, by whisking ingredients vigorously.) Prepare sauce and let stand for several hours before serving. It can also be refrigerated for a day or two in a tightly sealed container.

Pepper Sauce

Yield: 4 or more servings

3–4 black peppercorns
⅔ cup dry white wine
1 Tb wine vinegar
1 Tb minced shallot (or scallion)
pinch of thyme
1 small bay leaf
¾ cup demi-glace*
1 Tb chopped parsley
cayenne pepper
1½ Tb butter, softened

Crush peppercorns in a mortar, and combine with wine, vinegar, shallot, thyme, and bay leaf in a saucepan. Simmer rapidly over high heat until sauce has been reduced by two-thirds. Add demi-glace, and boil for a few seconds. Strain the sauce, then return it to the pan. Add parsley and a little cayenne pepper. Simmer a few minutes longer, remove from heat and stir in butter a bit at a time.

* Brown sauce, meat gravy, or beef bouillon slightly thickened with flour may be substituted for demi-glace.

Rémoulade Sauce

Yield: 4 or more servings

1 cup mayonnaise
1 Tb prepared mustard
1½ tsp minced capers
2 tsp sweet pickles, chopped
1½ tsp minced parsley
1 tsp chopped chervil (or pinch of dried)
1½ tsp chopped tarragon (or generous pinch of dried)
1½ tsp anchovy paste
dash of cayenne pepper

Combine all the ingredients, and continue stirring with a wooden spoon until thoroughly blended. Let sauce stand for an hour or two before serving.

Salsa Verde

Yield: 4 or more servings

½ cup chopped parsley
3 anchovy fillets, mashed
1 small boiled potato
2 Tb chopped dill pickle (or capers)
1 garlic clove, chopped
2 Tb chopped onion
1 Tb chopped basil (optional)
1 cup oil
2 Tb vinegar
salt and pepper

In a blender, combine all ingredients except salt and pepper; blend to a coarse purée. Taste for seasoning, and add salt and pepper accordingly.

Tartar Sauce

Yield: 4 or more servings

3 hard-cooked eggs
about ½ cup oil
1 Tb vinegar
1 Tb minced sweet pickles
1 Tb chopped capers
1 Tb minced parsley
salt and pepper

Mash egg yolks in a mixing bowl, and add oil slowly, alternating with drops of vinegar and whisking constantly. When sauce has thickened to mayonnaise consistency, add pickles, capers, and parsley. Season to taste with salt and pepper. (Optional variation: Press egg whites through a sieve, and add to sauce.)

Quick Tartar Sauce

Yield: 4 or more servings

1 cup mayonnaise
1 Tb vinegar
2 Tb minced parsley
1 tsp mustard
1 Tb sweet green pickle relish

Combine all ingredients in a mixing bowl or blender, and blend thoroughly.

Salsa Verde (p. 22)

Anchovy, Curry, and Maître d'Hôtel Butters (pp. 24–25)

Anchovy Butter

(Serve with steaks or spread on toast.)

¾ cup butter, softened
6 anchovy fillets, drained
juice of ½ lemon
1½ teaspoons minced parsley (optional)
dash of cayenne pepper

Cream the butter until light and fluffy. Mince anchovies, or pound them to a paste in a mortar. Blend anchovies, lemon juice, and parsley into butter. (All mixing may be done either by hand or with a food processor.) Season to taste with cayenne pepper, and beat until thoroughly blended. Store tightly covered in refrigerator.

Curry Butter

(Serve with lamb, fish, and vegetables.)

¾ cup butter, softened
½ to ¾ tsp curry powder
black or white pepper, freshly ground

Cream the butter until light and fluffy. Add curry powder and fresh ground pepper, blending well. (All mixing may be done either by hand or with a food processor.) Store tightly covered in refrigerator.

Garlic Butter

(Serve with grilled meats, or use in making garlic bread.)

6 garlic cloves
¾ cup butter, softened
pepper, freshly ground

Crush garlic in a mortar, and pound to a paste. Cream the butter, season lightly with pepper, and mix well with garlic paste until light and fluffy. (All mixing may be done either by hand or with a food processor.) To get a very smooth consistency, force garlic butter through a sieve before refrigerating. Store tightly covered in refrigerator.

Maître d'Hôtel Butter

(Serve with fish and steak.)

¾ cup butter, softened
juice of ½ lemon
3 Tb minced parsley
salt
pepper, freshly ground

Cream the butter, and blend in all the other ingredients. Beat until mixture is light and fluffy. (All mixing may be done either by hand or with a food processor.) Store tightly covered in refrigerator; apportioning the seasoned butter among individual small ramekins, covered with foil or plastic wrap, is a convenient way of storing it.

Mixed Herb Butter

(Serve with fish, chicken, meats, and vegetables.)

¾ *cup butter, softened*
2 Tb lemon juice
¼ *cup fresh minced herbs (e.g., tarragon, chives,*
  parsley, or a combination)
salt
pepper, freshly ground

Cream the butter until light and fluffy. Beat in lemon juice and herbs; season to taste with salt and fresh ground pepper. Blend thoroughly. (All mixing may be done either by hand or with a food processor.) Store tightly covered in refrigerator.

Mustard Butter

(Serve with chicken, organ meats, and steaks.)

¾ *cup butter, softened*
3 Tb prepared mustard (preferably Dijon)
salt
pepper, freshly ground
3 Tb minced chives (optional)

Cream the butter until light and fluffy. Gradually beat in mustard, mixing well after each addition. Add salt and fresh ground pepper to taste, then blend in chives. (All mixing may be done either by hand or with a food processor.) Store tightly covered in refrigerator.

Barbecued and Grilled Meats

Beef Kabob with Prunes

Yield: 4 servings

1½ lb lean beef (fillet or sirloin)
20 prunes
20 large mushroom caps
8 bay leaves
salt
black pepper, freshly ground
pinch of thyme leaves, crushed
oil
1 cup of white rice, cooked (optional)

Cut beef in 1½-inch cubes. Put prunes in a bowl, cover with warm water, and soak until needed. Wipe mushroom caps with a damp kitchen towel. On 4 skewers, alternate prunes, meat cubes, and mushroom caps; then put a bay leaf at each end of the skewers. Season with salt and fresh ground pepper, sprinkle with thyme, brush with oil, and grill over high heat, turning the skewers often and basting with more oil from time to time. The meat cubes should be lightly charred outside, and their centers done according to individual taste. (This dish may be served on a bed of cooked rice.)

Continental Cheeseburgers

Yield: 4 servings

2 lb lean ground beef
4 slices fontina (or Swiss) cheese
1–2 Tb prepared mustard
oil
black pepper, freshly ground
salt
2 Tb butter, softened
1 Tb anchovy paste

Divide ground beef in 8 portions, and form into patties. Trim slices of cheese to the same size and shape as the patties. Spread cheese with mustard, and put 1 slice between each pair of patties. Press gently with fingers to make the "sandwich" hold together, brush with oil, season with a little fresh ground pepper, and grill over a very hot charcoal fire for 5 minutes. Turn burgers, and sprinkle lightly with salt. Combine butter and anchovy paste, and dot surface of cheeseburgers with this mixture. Cook for about 5 minutes longer.

Beef Kabob with Prunes (p. 26)

Deviled Hamburgers (p. 28)

Deviled Hamburgers

Yield: 4 servings

1½ lb ground beef
3 Tb prepared mustard
2 Tb horseradish
1 small onion, minced
½ tsp Worcestershire sauce
¼ cup chili sauce
oil

Combine all ingredients except oil, and make 4 hamburger patties about ½ inch thick. Brush with oil, and place them on a hot grill. Brown well on both sides, turning only once and brushing occasionally with more oil. Serve on toasted sesame rolls.

Piquant Hamburgers with Onions

Yield: 4 servings

2 large onions, peeled
1½ lb ground beef
several sprigs parsley, chopped
1 egg
salt and pepper
3 Tb oil
2 Tb butter
Pepper Sauce or Curry Sauce (see Index)
1 large ripe tomato, sliced

Chop ½ of an onion, and slice the rest. Combine ground beef, chopped onion, parsley, egg, and a pinch of salt and pepper. Make 4 large, flattened hamburgers from the mixture, brush lightly with oil, and place on a hot grill. When nicely charred on one side, turn burgers and cook the other side, brushing with oil again.

Sauté sliced onions in butter, with a pinch of salt, until well cooked and nicely browned. Arrange hamburgers on a heated serving platter, pour sauce over them, top with sautéed onions, and garnish with tomato slices. (You may add additional garnish of lettuce leaves, thin slices of cucumbers, and scallions.)

Hamburgers with Smoked Ham

Yield: 4 servings

¼ lb cooked smoked ham
2 lb ground beef
2 egg yolks
salt and pepper
all-purpose flour
oil

Dice ham in very small cubes, and mix well with beef, egg yolks, and a pinch of salt and pepper.

Flour your hands, and make 8 hamburger patties about ½ inch thick. Brush them with oil, and place on a hot grill, browning well on both sides. Arrange on a heated platter, then serve piping hot, preferably with Marot Sauce or Mustard Butter (see Index).

Hamburgers with Sour Cream and Apples

Yield: 4 servings

½ lb onions
2 lb ground beef
8 Tb butter, melted
salt and pepper
pinch of nutmeg, freshly grated
all-purpose flour
1 cup sour cream
½ lb apples, sliced thin

Peel onions; chop ½ of an onion fine, and slice the rest. Mix beef with 1 tablespoon of melted butter, chopped onion, and a pinch each of salt, pepper, and nutmeg.

Make 8 hamburger patties, dust lightly with flour, brush with melted butter, and grill over high heat. When nicely charred on one side, turn and baste with 2 tablespoons of melted butter.

In a small saucepan, heat sour cream. Sauté sliced onions in 2 tablespoons of remaining butter, with a pinch of salt, until golden brown. Flour the apple slices lightly, and brown in remaining butter.

Put hamburgers on a serving platter, spread them with warm sour cream, top with chopped onions, and serve garnished with cooked onion and apple slices.

Zesty Hamburgers with Worcestershire

Yield: 4 servings

1½ lb ground beef
salt and pepper
Worcestershire sauce
4 Tb butter, melted
prepared brown mustard

Put ground beef in mixing bowl, and season with a pinch of salt and pepper and a few drops of Worcestershire sauce, according to taste. Mix well, and make 4 hamburger patties, about ½ inch thick. Brush with melted butter, and place on a hot grill. When burgers are nicely browned on one side, turn and baste them with melted butter, then finish cooking to taste. Serve with a pot of spicy brown mustard on the side.

English Grill Steaks

Yield: 4 servings

2 small beef or lamb steaks (about 1 to 1½ lb each)
3 Tb butter, melted
5 Tb butter, softened
1 tsp dry English mustard
salt
white pepper
cayenne pepper
1 tsp Worcestershire sauce
1 tsp mushroom ketchup*

Brush the steaks with melted butter, and grill them over a very hot fire. When charred on one side, turn steaks and finish cooking to individual taste. While steaks are cooking, combine softened butter, dry mustard, a pinch each of salt, white pepper, and cayenne pepper, the Worcestershire sauce, and mushroom ketchup, blending thoroughly.

Arrange steaks on a warmed serving platter, pour warm sauce over them, and serve.

* Mushroom ketchup is available in the gourmet section of many supermarkets and in specialty food stores.

Rum Marinated Filet Mignon

Yield: 4 servings

½ cup oil
½ cup rum
2 garlic cloves, minced
salt
pinch of oregano
½ tsp paprika
4 filets mignons (about ½ lb each)

Combine oil, rum, garlic, salt to taste, oregano, and paprika. Put steaks on a deep platter, pour seasoned mixture over them, and marinate for several hours, turning them often.

Drain steaks well, and pat dry. Reserve marinade. Grill over a very hot charcoal fire, basting occasionally with marinade. When properly cooked, the outside of the steaks should be nicely charred, while the center remains rare and juicy.

Tangy Filet Mignon with Gorgonzola

Yield: 4 servings

4 filets mignons (about ½ lb each)
about 2 Tb oil
pepper and salt
4 Tb butter, softened
2 oz mild Gorgonzola cheese
¼ cup chopped onion
1 tsp sharp Dijon mustard
watercress sprigs (optional)

Brush steaks lightly with oil, and season with pepper to taste. Cook for a few minutes on each side over a hot charcoal fire. Sprinkle with salt only when done.

While steaks are cooking, blend butter and Gorgonzola until smooth. Add chopped onion and mustard and mix well.

Arrange grilled steaks on a heated serving platter, spread the Gorgonzola butter over them, and serve immediately. (Sprigs of watercress would make an attractive, delicious garnish for the grilled meat.)

Florentine Steak

Yield: 4 servings

2 T-bone steaks, about 1½ inches thick
olive oil
black pepper, freshly ground
salt
2 lemons, cut in half

Rub steaks with a little oil and plenty of fresh ground black pepper, then let them absorb these condiments for a few minutes. Cook steaks on a grill over hot glowing coals, turning to cook both sides uniformly. Meat should be lightly charred outside and rare inside. Season with salt, and garnish with lemon halves to serve.

Piquant Hamburgers with Onions (p. 28)

Grilled Steak and Eggs

Yield: 4 servings

4 rib or club steaks (about ½ lb each)
3 Tb oil
2 lemons
2 Tb chopped parsley
salt
black pepper, freshly ground
4 eggs

Combine oil, juice of half a lemon, chopped parsley, and several turns of fresh ground black pepper. Marinate steaks in this mixture for about 30 minutes, turning them several times.

Drain and pat dry, then cook them on a very hot grill for 3 or 4 minutes on each side, according to individual taste. While grilling the second side, break an egg carefully atop each steak, and remove from heat when whites are well set. Serve immediately, garnished with remaining lemon cut in wedges.

Indonesian Steaks

Yield: 4 servings

4 small club steaks (about ½ lb each; or 2 lb
    lean chuck steak)
2 Tb soy sauce
¼ cup oil
¼ cup water
½ lb small white onions, peeled
½ lb green beans, trimmed
salt
6 Tb butter

Pound steaks lightly to tenderize. Blend soy sauce, oil, and water. Dredge steaks in this mixture, then marinate for about 1 hour, turning them occasionally.

Blanch onions in boiling water for 10 minutes. Cook green beans in lightly salted water, draining them while still slightly underdone. Sauté cooked onions and green beans in separate pans with 3 tablespoons of butter and a little salt in each.

Remove steaks from marinade, pat dry, and cook on grill over a hot fire, basting them occasionally with marinade. Season to taste with salt when done. Transfer steaks to a large heated serving platter, surround with cooked vegetables, and serve immediately.

London Broil

Yield: 4 to 6 servings

about 2½ lb flank steak
⅓ cup butter, melted
¼ cup dry red wine
salt
black pepper, freshly ground

Use only the best grade of flank steak for grilling. Remove tough outer membrane, and slash any fat around edges of the meat to keep it from curling.

Combine melted butter and wine, and brush steak with the mixture. Sear steak over hot fire. Baste often and turn only once during entire cooking period, about 8 to 10 minutes. Collect drippings while cooking. When meat is charred outside but still quite rare inside, season with salt and pepper, cut in long diagonal slices, and serve with wine-butter drippings poured over them. For those who prefer their grilled meat medium or well-done, longer cooking time and more frequent turning of the meat is recommended (see Introduction).

Marinated Club Steak Béarnaise

Yield: 4 servings

¼ cup minced parsley
3–4 fresh sage leaves, minced (or ¼ tsp dried,
  crushed)
pinch of rosemary
½ cup oil
2 Tb vinegar
4 boneless club steaks (about 6–8 oz each; or 2 lb
  lean chuck steak)
salt and pepper
1 bunch watercress, washed and trimmed
Béarnaise Sauce (see Index)

Combine parsley, sage, rosemary, oil, and vinegar, and mix well. Pound steaks to flatten slightly, and place them on a large platter. Pour marinade over steaks, and set aside to marinate for at least 1 hour, turning them occasionally.

Drain steaks, dry them well, and grill over high heat. When they are slightly charred on one side, turn and char them on the other. When done to taste, season with salt and pepper and serve piping hot, garnished generously with watercress. Serve accompanied with Béarnaise Sauce.

Pepper Steak Flambé

Yield: 4 servings

about 2 doz peppercorns
oil
4 club or rib steaks (about ½ lb each)
salt
6 Tb brandy (or kirsch), warmed

Crush peppercorns in a mortar. Coat steaks lightly with oil, sprinkle well with crushed pepper, and rub in with your hand to make sure pepper adheres to the meat. Let stand for about 1 hour.

Grill steaks over high heat, turning them only once. The meat should be lightly charred on the outside, and rare to medium-rare toward the center.

Remove cooked steaks from grill, sprinkle with salt to taste, and arrange on a heated serving platter. Pour warm brandy over steaks, and ignite with a match. Serve immediately, while still flaming.

Rib Steak Bercy

Yield: 4 servings

For the Bercy Butter:
5 oz beef marrow
⅓ cup dry white wine
1 shallot, chopped (or 2 scallions without green tops)
4 Tb butter, softened
2 Tb chopped parsley
salt
black pepper, freshly ground
juice of ½ lemon

For grilling:
4 rib steaks (about ½ lb each)
2 Tb butter, melted
salt and pepper
2–3 Tb meat extract* (or roast beef gravy)

To prepare the Bercy Butter: Chop beef marrow in small pieces, and blanch for 10 minutes in lightly salted boiling water. Drain and reserve marrow. Pour wine into a saucepan, and add chopped shallot. Bring to a boil, then simmer to reduce by half. Remove from heat, mix in softened butter a bit at a time, beef marrow, and chopped parsley. Season to taste with salt and pepper, and add lemon juice. Set this mixture aside.

Brush rib steaks with melted butter, and grill over a hot charcoal fire, turning them only once. When done, steaks should be charred on the outside and rare inside. Remove from heat, and season with salt and pepper to taste. Coat with meat extract or beef gravy from roast and serve; pass around the warmed Bercy Butter in a sauceboat.

*Meat extract is available in the gourmet section of many supermarkets and in specialty food stores.

Rib Steak Charolais

Yield: 4 servings

7 Tb butter
2–3 Tb chopped onion
3 Tb all-purpose flour
1 cup dry red wine
2 garlic cloves, minced
1 cup tomato purée
2–3 Tb Madeira wine (or Marsala)
salt and pepper
4 rib steaks (about ½ lb each)

Melt 5 tablespoons of butter in a small saucepan over low heat. Add onion, and sauté until transparent. Add flour and cook briefly, stirring constantly. Stir in wine, raise heat, and bring to a boil. Add garlic, tomato purée, wine, and salt and pepper to taste. Reduce heat and simmer for about 30 minutes.

Melt remaining 2 tablespoons of butter, and brush it on the meat. Grill steaks over a hot fire, turning them only once; char the outside while keeping center rare. Transfer to a serving platter, season to taste with salt and pepper, and cover with tomato sauce.

Sirloin Maître d'Hôtel

Yield: 4 servings

2 sirloin steaks (at least 1 lb each)
salt and pepper
Maître d'Hôtel Butter (see Index)

Grill steaks over very hot coals to char lightly on both sides. Cook for 2 or 3 minutes, or longer, watching carefully until they are done to individual taste. Cut steaks in half, season lightly with salt and pepper, and serve accompanied with Maître d'Hôtel Butter.

Grilled Steak and Eggs (p. 32)

Veal Rolls with Cheese (p. 37)

Grilled Veal Chops

Yield: 4 servings

4 large veal chops (6–8 oz each)
4 Tb butter, melted
salt and pepper
2 lemons, cut in wedges

Pound chops briefly with a mallet or the flat side of a cleaver to tenderize. Remove bone. Brush chops with melted butter, and set on hot grill. Cook for about 15 minutes, basting occasionally with melted butter and turning chops only once. Season to taste with salt and pepper. Serve with lemon wedges. (French-fried potatoes are a good side dish for grilled chops.)

Roast Veal on the Spit

Yield: 6 servings

½ cup melted butter
½ cup dry white wine
4–5 lb veal loin, boned and rolled
salt
¼ cup heavy cream
pepper, freshly ground
chopped parsley

Combine melted butter and wine. Fasten the meat on the spit, and brush with butter-wine mixture. Roast very slowly over medium-hot grill, basting continually with butter and wine. Allow about 18 to 20 minutes per pound of meat. Season to taste with salt when half-done.

When meat is cooked, prepare a gravy by combining heavy cream with the hot drippings. If necessary, season with fresh ground pepper and additional salt. Serve the gravy with chopped parsley in a sauceboat.

Roast Stuffed Breast of Veal

Yield: 6 to 8 servings

½ lb ground veal
½ lb pork (or Italian sweet) sausage
1 onion, minced
1 garlic clove, minced
2 Tb chopped parsley
¼ cup brandy (or red wine or meat broth)
salt and pepper
1 egg
½ cup bread crumbs
4–5 lb boned breast of veal
melted butter for basting

In a large bowl, combine veal, sausage meat without casings, onion, garlic, parsley, brandy, and a pinch of salt and pepper. Mix well. Add egg and bread crumbs, and blend thoroughly.

Flatten breast of veal, and put the stuffing in the center. Fold veal in half, and sew up sides with strong cooking twine. Truss veal roast securely with butcher's cord, and fasten carefully on the spit so that stuffing will not seep out during cooking. Brush with a little melted butter, and cook very slowly over medium heat for 2 to 2½ hours, or until tender. Center should still be juicy and slightly pink when done. (This dish is also excellent when served cold, with a tangy Salsa Verde; see Index.)

Skewered Veal and Mushrooms

Yield: 4 servings

2 lb boneless veal (preferably cut from leg)
½ lb slab bacon
½ cup oil
juice of 1 lemon
⅓ cup chopped parsley
salt and pepper
1 lb fresh mushrooms

Cut veal and bacon in bite-size cubes. Combine oil, lemon juice, chopped parsley, and salt and pepper to taste. Marinate veal and bacon in this mixture for 2 hours. Wash and trim mushrooms, separating caps from stems. (Reserve stems for use in other dishes.)

Drain and pat dry veal and bacon cubes, reserving the marinade. On long skewers, alternate veal cubes with bacon and mushroom caps. Brush with a little marinade, and grill over high heat until well browned. While meat is cooking, turn skewers often and baste continually with marinade. When well done, season to taste with salt and pepper, preferably fresh ground.

Veal Rolls with Cheese

Yield: 4 servings

8 thin slices veal
2 medium-size onions
bread crumbs
1 cup grated Parmesan cheese
oil
salt and pepper
8 slices fontina cheese
bay leaves

Tenderize veal by pounding lightly with a meat pounder. Chop ½ onion, and combine in a bowl with bread crumbs, grated Parmesan, 2 tablespoons of oil, and salt and pepper to taste. Mix well. Spread this stuffing on veal slices, and cover each with a slice of fontina. Cut remaining onion in thick slices. Roll veal, tucking in the ends so that stuffing will not seep out, and thread on skewers, alternating each veal roll with a slice of onion and a bay leaf. Brush generously with oil, and grill over high heat. (Serve with a mixed green salad, preferably with a vinaigrette or mustard-base dressing.)

Barbecued Lamb Shoulder

Yield: 6 to 8 servings

3 garlic cloves
10 peppercorns
several sprigs of rosemary
salt
3½ to 4 lb lamb shoulder, boned

Crush garlic, peppercorns, and rosemary together. Add salt, and rub seasoning mixture over inner side of meat thoroughly. Roll lamb, tie with butcher's cord, and rub remaining mixture on outside. Let stand for about 1 hour. Fasten the lamb on the spit, and roast over a hot fire, basting frequently with salted water. For rare meat, cook about 15 minutes for every pound (at 140°F on a meat thermometer). Allow cooked meat to set briefly before serving from a large carving board.

Lamb on the Spit

Yield: 6 servings

4- or 5-lb leg of lamb (preferably including rack
   and kidneys)
4 garlic cloves, slivered
4 sprigs rosemary, chopped
½ cup olive oil
2–3 Tb vinegar
salt
black pepper, freshly ground

Make deep slits in meat with a sharp kitchen knife, and insert garlic slivers and rosemary.

Combine oil, vinegar, salt, and a few turns of fresh ground pepper. Pour mixture over leg of lamb, and marinate for about 2 hours, turning the meat occasionally.

Drain lamb and pat dry, reserving the marinade, then fasten the meat on the spit. Roast for about 1 to 1½ hours, preferably over hot charcoal fire, basting occasionally with marinade. Cook until meat is well browned and crisp on the outside, but still juicy and slightly pink in the center.

Leg of Lamb French Style

Yield: 4 to 6 servings

1 small leg of lamb (about 3½ to 4 lb)
2 garlic cloves, slivered
salt and pepper
melted butter
Marot Sauce (see Index)

Cut slits in the meat, and insert garlic. Season with salt and pepper, then brush with melted butter. Fasten the leg of lamb on the spit, and roast over high heat, basting occasionally with melted butter. French-style lamb should be prepared rather rare, that is, cooked only for about 15 minutes per pound of meat. Serve very hot. Marot Sauce is an excellent accompaniment.

Persian Grilled Lamb

Yield: 4 servings

2- or 3-lb boneless leg of lamb
pinch of mixed spices (e.g. marjoram, thyme,
   rosemary)
oil
4 medium-size tomatoes
salt
vinegar
chopped chervil
2 medium-size red onions, sliced thin

Rub leg of lamb with mixed spices and oil, then set on grill over hot fire to cook. Baste with additional oil from time to time. Turn meat several times while grilling. About 15 or 20 minutes before meat is finished cooking, cut tomatoes in half, squeeze lightly to extract juice and seeds, brush with a little oil, and set them around the edges of the grill to cook along with the lamb.

When meat is fork-tender, cut in slices. Arrange on a warmed serving platter together with cooked tomato halves. Sprinkle salt and a few drops of vinegar over both meat and tomatoes, and then garnish with chopped chervil. Surround with raw onion slices to serve.

Lamb on the Spit (p. 38)

Roasted Leg of Lamb with Garlic-Anchovy Paste

Yield: 8 servings

4- to 5-lb leg of lamb
15 garlic cloves
4 anchovy fillets, minced
melted butter
salt and pepper
¼ cup lamb (or chicken) broth

Have butcher remove skin and trim outer fat from leg of lamb and cut off end of the bone. Mince 3 garlic cloves and combine with anchovies; insert paste into slits cut in meat. Brush leg of lamb with butter, fasten on the spit, and roast over a very hot charcoal fire for about 1½ hours. Baste occasionally with melted butter, and when almost done, season with salt and pepper.

Peel and boil remaining dozen of garlic cloves in a small amount of salted water and drain. Combine garlic-flavored water in a bowl with 1 cup of meat drippings and the broth. Boil over high heat to reduce the liquid. Serve the meat well done, together with the light gravy in a sauceboat. (Roasted sweet peppers on wooden skewers is recommended as an accompaniment.)

Savory Leg of Lamb on the Spit

Yield: 4 to 6 servings

1 small leg of lamb (about 3½ to 4 lb)
1 stalk celery, cut in thin strips
sweet pickles, cut in thin spears
5-6 anchovy fillets, split lengthwise
salt
oil

Lift up the skin of the leg of lamb without detaching it entirely, and press underneath the strips of celery and pickles and the anchovy fillets. Season with salt, and pat skin back into position. Tie meat with butcher's cord, and brush with a little oil. Fasten the leg of lamb on the spit, and roast over a hot charcoal fire until done medium-rare, allowing about 15 minutes of cooking time per pound of meat.

Serve while still very hot, together with a side dish of cooked navy beans tossed with drippings from the roast.

Lamb Chops with Mint

Yield: 4 servings

8 mint sprigs
½ cup vinegar
1 tsp sugar
salt and pepper
8 loin lamb chops

Trim and mince 4 mint sprigs. Combine these with vinegar, sugar, and salt and pepper to taste. Put lamb chops on a large platter, pour the mixture over them, and marinate for 1 hour, turning chops from time to time.

Let charcoal fire burn until reduced to hot coals. Throw remaining mint sprigs directly on the fire. Grill lamb chops over the mint-scented coals for 5 minutes on each side, turning them only once. Serve immediately.

Baby Lamb Chops with Tomatoes Parmesan

Yield: 4 servings

4 firm ripe tomatoes, cut in half
grated Parmesan cheese
4 tsp butter
2 lb baby lamb chops
2 Tb lard, melted
salt
black pepper, freshly ground

Sprinkle tomatoes with grated Parmesan, and dot each half with ½ teaspoon of butter. Grill tomato halves toward edges of the grill until tender but still rather firm.

Meanwhile, brush lamb chops lightly on both sides with lard. Season with salt and a little fresh ground pepper, and place them on grill. Cook over a hot charcoal fire, turning chops often as they cook. Heap grilled chops on a heated platter, and surround with tomatoes to serve.

Lamb Kabob with Yogurt

Yield: 4 servings

2 to 2½ lb boned leg of lamb (or shoulder)
1 onion, chopped coarse
6 Tb oil
salt
1½ lb firm ripe tomatoes
1 Tb butter
¼ cup butter, melted
4 thick slices bread
1 cup yogurt, heated

Cut lamb in 1-inch cubes, then make a layer of cubes on a platter. Spread chopped onion over the meat. Sprinkle with oil, season with salt, and marinate for about 1 hour, turning pieces occasionally.

Reserve 2 medium-size tomatoes, and peel, seed, and chop the rest. In a saucepan, melt 1 tablespoon of butter, add chopped tomatoes and a pinch of salt, and simmer until tomatoes are reduced to a fairly thick purée.

Toast bread on grill, cut into croutons, and put them on a hot platter. Pour 2 or 3 tablespoons of melted butter over croutons and keep warm.

Drain marinade from meat, and thread meat cubes on skewers. Cook on a very hot grill, turning and basting often with remaining melted butter. Cut the reserved tomatoes in half crosswise, salt lightly, and grill. Spread tomato purée over croutons, and cover with heated yogurt. Place barbecued meat cubes on top, and surround with grilled tomatoes to serve.

41

Marinated Lamb and Tomato Kabob

Yield: 4 servings

2 to 2½ lb lamb (preferably cut from leg)
½ cup dry white wine
juice of 1 lemon
1 tsp cumin
1 tsp fennel seed
½ onion, chopped
pinch of ground ginger
pinch of sugar
2 Tb soy sauce
salt and pepper
2 lb cherry (or plum) tomatoes
1 lb medium-wide egg noodles*

Cut meat in 1½-inch cubes. Combine wine, lemon juice, cumin, fennel, onion, ginger, sugar, soy sauce, and salt and pepper to taste. Mix well, and pour over the meat. Marinate lamb for about 2 hours, turning the cubes occasionally.

Drain the meat cubes, reserving marinade. Dip tomatoes in marinade, then thread meat cubes and tomatoes alternately on fine skewers. Grill over hot coals, preferably from a wood fire. Turn skewers often as they are cooking, basting them occasionally with marinade. Continue grilling until lamb cubes are nicely browned, but still have slightly pink centers. Serve immediately on the skewers, on a bed of cooked egg noodles.

*Noodles can be precooked *al dente* and reheated in a pot of simmering water set near the edge of the grill, or else can be cooked in water boiled directly over the grill.

Frankfurters with Cheese Stuffing

Yield: 4 servings

8 frankfurters
3 Tb grated Parmesan cheese
3 Tb finely shredded mozzarella cheese
1 small tomato, chopped
¼ tsp oregano
1 Tb chopped basil
salt and pepper
8 bacon slices

Slit frankfurters deeply lengthwise, but do not cut all the way through. In a bowl, combine Parmesan, mozzarella, chopped tomato, oregano, and basil. Sprinkle lightly with salt and pepper to taste, and blend well.

Spread frankfurters with the mixture, and close tightly by winding bacon around them in a spiral and securing well with toothpicks. Grill over hot coals, turning often until bacon is browned and crisp.

Grilled Knackwurst with Bacon

Yield: 4 servings

8 knackwurst
prepared mustard
horseradish (optional)
8 slices bacon

Slice knackwurst nearly in half lengthwise—leaving about a quarter inch of casing and meat stuffing intact at one end. Spread inside surfaces with mustard and horseradish to taste. Join halves together by wrapping a slice of bacon in spiral fashion around each knackwurst, securing cut end with toothpicks in several places to keep filling from oozing out. Grill sausages until bacon is browned and crisp.

Marinated Calf's Liver (p. 44)

Roasted Leg of Lamb with Garlic-Anchovy Paste (p. 40)

Grilled Veal Kidneys

Yield: 4 servings

1½ lb veal kidneys
½ cup oil
juice of ½ lemon
salt and pepper
2 or 3 lemons, cut in quarters

Remove outer membrane, and split kidneys in half. Remove veins and fat, then wash thoroughly and drain. Combine oil, lemon juice, salt and pepper; marinate kidneys in the mixture for about 30 minutes, turning them occasionally. Drain off and reserve marinade.

Cook kidneys on a medium-hot grill, turning often and basting them with marinade. Remember that kidneys should be cooked slowly but not too long, since excessive cooking will toughen them. When done, they should be nicely browned, yet have slightly pink centers. Serve with lemon wedges.

Grilled Calf's Liver

Yield: 4 servings

4 slices calf's or beef liver (about 1½ lb)
2 tsp oil
salt and pepper
Béarnaise Sauce (see Index)

Brush liver lightly with oil, and grill over medium heat for 8 to 10 minutes. Sprinkle with salt and pepper. During the last few minutes of cooking, lower grill closer to heat to produce a light crust. Serve piping hot, accompanied with Béarnaise Sauce.

Calf's Liver with Onions

Yield: 4 servings

2 medium-size onions, sliced thin
2 Tb butter
4 slices bacon
4 slices calf's or beef liver (about 1½ lb)
2 tsp oil
salt and pepper

Sauté sliced onions in butter until transparent. In a separate pan, fry bacon until crisp. Brush liver slices lightly with oil, place on a hot grill, and cook over medium heat for 8 to 10 minutes. During the last few minutes of cooking, lower grill closer to heat to produce a light crust.

Arrange grilled liver on a warmed serving platter, season to taste with salt and pepper, and cover with sautéed onions. Crumble bacon on top, then serve piping hot.

Marinated Calf's Liver

Yield: 4 servings

⅓ cup dry red wine
⅓ cup oil
2 garlic cloves, minced
salt and pepper
4 thick slices calf's or beef liver (1½ to 2 lb)

Combine wine, oil, minced garlic, and a pinch of salt and pepper. Put liver slices on a plate, and pour marinade over them; set aside to marinate for about 2 hours.

Drain and reserve marinade. Put liver on a hot grill, and cook over medium heat for 8 to 10 minutes, basting occasionally with marinade. During the last few minutes of cooking, lower grill closer to heat to produce a light crust.

Grilled Italian Sausages

Yield: 4 to 6 servings

8 or 12 Italian hot (or sweet) sausages
Dijon mustard

Cut sausages in half lengthwise, but leaving them linked. Spread generously with mustard. Set sausages on a hot grill, with their cut inner side downward to keep from curling while cooking. Cook until crisp and very well done, turning them only once. Serve piping hot. (Accompany with roasted or mashed potatoes and foil-roasted apples. Additional spicy mustard is also recommended for serving.)

Mixed Grill

Yield: 4 servings

2 thin slices beef fillet (about 1 lb)
4 thin slices calf's liver (about 1 lb)
4 slices pork fillet (about 1 lb; or 4 pork sausages)
8 small kidneys (optional)
4 lamb chops (preferably baby chops)
melted butter (or oil)
salt and pepper

Brush all cuts of meat with melted butter or oil, and sear on hot grill to seal in juices. When nicely browned on one side, turn each piece of meat and cook to taste on the other side. (Smaller pieces should be seared more briefly over the hottest part of the grill; larger cuts should be cooked longer over medium heat.) The pork should be tender, but well cooked through. Baste all meats with a little melted butter or oil as needed.

When meats are done, season to taste with salt and pepper, and serve with any of various grilled vegetables (see Index), together with spicy brown mustard and prepared tangy barbecue or steak sauces to use as dips.

Sausage and Beef Fantasy

Yield: 4 servings

1 lb lean beef (fillet or sirloin)
1 lb (sweet or hot) Italian sausages
12 mushroom caps
12 plum (or cherry) tomatoes
12 small onions, peeled
1 garlic clove, minced
½ cup oil
salt
Pepper Sauce or Curry Sauce (see Index)

Cut beef and sausages into bite-size pieces. Clean and soak mushrooms and tomatoes in cold water briefly. On long skewers, alternate 2 chunks of beef, 2 slices of sausage, 2 mushroom caps, 2 tomatoes, and 2 onions, until all ingredients are used up. Mix garlic, oil, and salt, and brush this mixture on the skewered meat and vegetables. Grill skewers over hot charcoal embers, turning them often and basting with marinade as needed until both meat and vegetables are nicely browned. Serve with either Pepper Sauce or Curry Sauce on the side.

Barbecued Spareribs with Savory Toast

Yield: 4 to 6 servings

4 lb spareribs
¼ cup lard, melted
salt and pepper
8 or 12 thick slices firm-textured, home-style bread

Brush spareribs lightly with melted lard. Sprinkle with salt and pepper, and cook on a hot grill, turning them occasionally and basting with melted lard. When spareribs seem about half-done, put slices of bread on top of them to toast and absorb some cooking juices. When meat is tender and cooked through, arrange toast on a large serving platter, and top with spareribs. (Ribs can be accompanied with an assortment of prepared barbecue and steak sauces for individual service.)

Sweet and Sour Spareribs

Yield: 4 to 6 servings

½ cup flat beer
2 Tb cider vinegar
1 Tb Worcestershire sauce
¾ cup chili sauce
1 Tb lemon juice
½ cup dark brown sugar, firmly packed
4 lb spareribs

Combine beer, vinegar, Worcestershire and chili sauces, lemon juice, and brown sugar in a saucepan. Cook over medium heat until sugar dissolves. Keep mixture warm.

Brush spareribs with the warm sauce, and grill over a hot fire, turning them occasionally and basting generously with sauce. Cooked ribs should be dark brown and well done, served well-glazed with sauce.

Barbecued Spareribs with Savory Toast (p. 46)

Sweetbreads with Maître d'Hôtel Butter

Yield: 4 servings

1 to 1½ lb veal sweetbreads
salt
½ cup butter, melted
Maître d'Hôtel Butter (see Index)

Clean sweetbreads by soaking in cold water for 1 hour. Transfer to a saucepan, and cover with fresh water. Salt lightly, bring to a boil, and simmer for about 5 minutes. Drain, rinse with cold water, pat dry, wrap in a clean dish towel, and weight down with a cutting board. Let stand for 2 hours or more, then cut in thick slices.

Brush sweetbreads with a little melted butter, and grill them on a hot fire, basting occasionally with melted butter. Serve accompanied with Maître d'Hôtel Butter.

Breaded Beef Tongue

Yield: 6 to 8 servings

1 fresh beef tongue (about 3½ to 4 lb)
1 Tb salt
1 small onion, sliced
1 stalk celery, sliced
1 carrot, sliced
bread crumbs
Dijon mustard
melted butter
Pepper Sauce (see Index)

Put tongue in a large kettle. Add salt, onion, celery, and carrot. Cover with cold water. Bring to a boil, reduce heat, and simmer until tender, about 2 to 3 hours. Remove tongue from water and cool slightly. Toast bread crumbs lightly.

Cut bones and gristle from thick end of tongue, and strip off the skin. Slice tongue thin. Spread slices of tongue with a light layer of mustard, dip in melted butter, then in toasted bread crumbs, and again in melted butter. Arrange tongue slices on hot grill, and cook until nicely browned, turning them frequently. Serve with Pepper Sauce.

Wild Hare on the Spit

Yield: 4 servings

1 hare (or large rabbit)
½ tsp fennel seeds, crushed
1 sprig thyme, minced (or ¼ tsp thyme leaves, crushed)
¼ cup butter, softened
salt and pepper
oil
2 lemons, cut in wedges

If hare has not been cleaned and prepared by a butcher, clean and wash thoroughly in cold running water, removing inner organs, head, and paws. Combine fennel seeds, thyme, and butter, mixing well.

Season hare inside and out with salt and pepper, stuff with seasoned butter mixture, and brush with oil. Tie legs together, and fasten the hare on the spit. Roast slowly over medium-hot fire until well browned and skin is very crispy, basting it occasionally with pan drippings. When done, carve in serving pieces, and arrange on a platter. Pour drippings over meat, and garnish with lemon wedges.

Down-Home Ham Steaks

Yield: 4 servings

4 medium-size ham steaks
milk
cloves
⅓ cup brown sugar
pineapple slices and juice

Soak ham steaks for a few hours in well-watered milk to extract excess salt. (Some cooks prefer the flavor of a beer or ginger ale bath.) Remove and drain ham steaks, then crisscross lightly with a sharp knife. Insert a generous number of cloves in the slits, on the top side only.

Make a runny paste of brown sugar, a few tablespoons of pineapple juice, and water. Coat ham steaks lightly with sugar mixture, then grill on oiled aluminum foil over a medium-hot fire, basting continually with the sugary paste. Turn slices only once, starting with the clove-spiked side up. Grill for 10 minutes or longer per side. Garnish with pineapple rings, which can be basted and lightly browned on the foil a few minutes before serving.

Savory Grilled Ham

Yield: 4 servings

4 thick slices smoked ham
8 cloves
several sprigs of rosemary
oil
4 tsp prepared barbecue sauce (or mustard)

Lightly cut a few slits in ham slices, then insert 2 cloves and crush and rub a little rosemary on one side of each slice of ham. Brush slices with oil, and spread with barbecue sauce, or mustard. Grill ham until nicely browned on one side, then turn to finish cooking on other side. Serve very hot, with a garnish of fresh ripe tomato slices and dill pickle spears.

Grilled Pig's Feet

Yield: 4 servings

4 pig's feet
1 tsp salt
1 onion
1 carrot
1 stalk celery
melted butter (or lard)
buttered bread crumbs

Scrub pig's feet thoroughly, then hold over an open flame for a few seconds if necessary to burn off remaining bristles. Remove any excess fat. Put pig's feet in a saucepan, and add cold, lightly salted water to cover. Bring to a boil, and skim off residue. Add onion, carrot, and celery. Cover and simmer for about 3 hours, or until meat comes off the bone easily.

Drain and set aside to cool. Dry pig's feet well, brush with melted butter, and roll them in bread crumbs.

Grill over medium-hot heat, turning them only once and brushing occasionally with melted butter, until meat is golden brown and crusty. (Creamy mashed potatoes are a good traditional side dish for grilled pig's feet.)

Roast Suckling Pig

Yield: 10 to 12 servings

10- to 12-lb suckling pig
1 cup oil
salt and pepper
6 garlic cloves, chopped
1 Tb mixed chopped herbs (rosemary, thyme,
   parsley)

Have your butcher prepare the pig for roasting, leaving head and tail intact. Combine oil, salt, pepper, garlic, and mixed herbs. Rub the cavity well with some of the seasoned oil. Sew opening, and fasten the pig very carefully on the spit. Roast over medium heat, preferably on an aromatic wood fire (olive, juniper, etc.), or over natural charcoal fire.

Baste continually with herbed oil and meat drippings. The pig will require about 3 hours' cooking time (170°F on a meat thermometer). When skin is crisp and meat is fork-tender, remove pig from spit and serve from a long wooden platter, carving as needed.

Sauced Pork Loin on the Spit

Yield: 4 servings

2- to 2½-lb pork loin
3–4 cloves
2 Tb soy sauce
½ cup oil
1 Tb prepared mustard
juice of 1 lemon
black pepper, freshly ground
salt

Stud pork loin with cloves. Mix soy sauce with oil, mustard, lemon juice, and plenty of fresh ground black pepper. Rub meat with mixture, and fasten loin on the spit. Roast over a very hot fire until meat is nicely browned. Reduce heat and continue cooking, basting occasionally with remaining sauce and pan drippings.

When meat is fork-tender and well done (170°F on a meat thermometer), sprinkle with salt to taste and serve. (Roasted potatoes or roasted corn on the cob are suitable side dishes, as well as Nut-Filled Baked Apples; see Index.)

Grilled Pig's Feet (p. 49)

Barbecued Chicken with Grilled Bacon, Tomatoes, and Mushrooms

Yield: 4 servings

*1 medium-size roasting chicken (about 3½
   to 4 lb)*
salt and pepper
½ cup butter, melted
1 Tb prepared mustard
bread crumbs
8 strips bacon
4 firm ripe tomatoes
oil
½ lb fresh mushrooms, sliced
1 lemon, sliced
Rémoulade Sauce (see Index)

Split chicken down the back, and clean and rinse well. Flatten the two halves with a meat pounder or flat side of a cleaver. Discard as many small bones as possible. Season to taste with salt and pepper, brush with melted butter, and grill over a very hot fire until skin is golden brown and crispy, turning and basting occasionally with melted butter. A few minutes before chicken is done, spread mustard on it, sprinkle with bread crumbs, and finish cooking.

Meanwhile, grill the bacon strips. Cut tomatoes in half crosswise, squeeze out juice and seeds, sprinkle with a little oil and salt, then grill until just tender. Sauté sliced mushrooms in a little melted butter, and salt them lightly. Place chicken on a serving platter, cover with bacon slices, and arrange cooked tomatoes and mushrooms around it. Garnish with lemon slices, and accompany with Rémoulade Sauce in a sauceboat.

Breaded Broiled Chicken

Yield: 4 servings

4 small broiler chickens, quartered
salt
melted butter
toasted bread crumbs for dredging
Tartar Sauce (see Index)

Clean and rinse chicken parts. Drain and pat dry. Season with salt, brush with melted butter, and dredge in toasted bread crumbs. Brush again with melted butter, and grill over medium heat until breading and skin become golden brown. Move grill closer to heat toward end of cooking to char skin slightly. Serve with Tartar Sauce in a sauceboat. (A mixed green salad with vinaigrette or mustard-base dressing would be a suitable accompaniment.)

Deviled Chicken

Yield: 4 servings

1 broiler chicken (about 3½ to 4 lb)
olive oil
salt
hot pepper flakes
1 lemon, cut in wedges

Clean and rinse chicken, then butterfly by splitting the breastbone and leaving the backbone intact. Flatten slightly with a meat pounder or flat side of a cleaver, taking care not to smash bones. Brush with oil, and sprinkle lightly with salt and hot pepper flakes.

Grill chicken over high heat, turning and brushing it occasionally with oil. Cook until it is well browned and has a crispy skin. Serve garnished with lemon wedges.

Gourmand Grilled Chicken

Yield: 4 servings

2 broiler chickens (about 2½ lb each)
⅓ cup tomato sauce
⅓ cup olive oil
2–3 scallions, chopped
pinch of sugar
pinch of oregano
salt
cayenne pepper

Clean and rinse chickens, then cut in quarters. Combine tomato sauce, olive oil, scallions, sugar, oregano, and salt to taste. Dip the chicken quarters in this marinade, coating them well.

Grill chicken over medium-hot coals, turning pieces often and basting occasionally with reserved marinade, for 12 to 15 minutes on each side. This dish goes well with Grilled Tomatoes (see Index).

Herbed Chicken on the Spit

Yield: 4 servings

3½- to 4-lb roasting chicken
8 Tb butter
1 Tb mixed herbs (chopped parsley, basil, oregano)
salt and pepper
¼ cup dry white wine

Clean and rinse chicken thoroughly in cold water. Cream 5 tablespoons of butter. Stir in mixed herbs, and season to taste with salt and pepper. Stuff cavity with about 3 tablespoons of herbed butter, and sew up the opening with cooking twine.

Spread remaining herbed butter over chicken, truss the bird, and fasten it on the spit. Season with salt and pepper, and roast over high heat. Melt remaining 3 tablespoons of butter, and mix with wine. Baste chicken often with the mixture and pan drippings. When chicken skin is golden brown and crisp, and flesh is tender, serve immediately.

53

Italian Country-Style Chicken

Yield: 4 servings

3½- to 4-lb roasting chicken
1 tsp minced sage
1 tsp minced rosemary
oil
6 oz prosciutto (or baked ham), sliced
2 garlic cloves, minced
salt and pepper

Clean chicken, rinse well, and drain. Set on a platter, combine half the sage and rosemary, and sprinkle over chicken. Brush with oil, and marinate for a couple of hours.

Mince half the prosciutto, and mix with garlic and remaining sage and rosemary. Season with salt and pepper. Stuff chicken with the prosciutto-garlic mixture, and sew up the opening. Wrap chicken in remaining slices of prosciutto, and tie with cooking twine. Fasten the bird on the spit, and roast over medium fire until skin is well browned and crisp. If necessary, remove outer prosciutto slices to allow for better browning. (Serve on a platter along with roasted potatoes and a ring of ripe tomato slices.)

Stuffed Chicken Roasted on the Spit

Yield: 4 servings

3½- to 4-lb roasting chicken
¼ lb lean bacon
2 anchovy fillets, minced
salt and pepper
½ lb Italian sweet sausage
1 truffle (optional)
¼ cup butter, melted
Tartar Sauce (or Mustard Sauce; see Index)

Clean chicken and soak in cold running water briefly. Cut bacon in strips. Cut small slits in chicken skin, and insert bacon and anchovies. Salt lightly and rub with pepper inside and out. Remove sausage from casing. Dice truffle, and mix with sausage meat. Stuff chicken with sausage mixture, and sew up opening. Truss bird securely, and fasten it on the spit.

Roast chicken over a medium-hot charcoal fire, basting occasionally with melted butter, until skin is crisp and well browned and stuffing is fully cooked. Serve with Tartar Sauce or with Mustard Sauce.

Breaded Chicken Livers

Yield: 4 servings

1 to 1½ lb chicken livers
pinch of mixed herbs (e.g. thyme, rosemary, sage)
2 Tb Marsala
salt and pepper
all-purpose flour
4 Tb butter, melted
bread crumbs for dredging
Pepper Sauce (see Index)

Season livers with mixed herbs, toss with Marsala, and marinate for 30 minutes. Drain livers, pat dry, season with salt and pepper, and dust with flour. Brush livers lightly with melted butter, dip in bread crumbs, and brush again with melted butter.

Cook breaded livers over a hot charcoal fire for about 3 minutes on each side. (They may also be grilled on well-oiled aluminum foil over hot fire, requiring a somewhat longer cooking time to brown nicely.)

Marinated Duckling (p. 56)

Marinated Duckling

Yield: 4 servings

2 small ducklings (or broiling chickens)
6 Tb oil
3 Tb red wine vinegar
3–4 fresh sage leaves, chopped (or pinch of dried)
2 garlic cloves, minced
1 cup chopped onions
salt
black pepper, freshly ground

Clean ducklings thoroughly and quarter them, washing in several changes of cold water. Drain and dry them carefully, then set aside.

Combine oil, vinegar, sage, garlic, onions, and salt and pepper to taste. Pour mixture over ducklings, and marinate for 2 to 3 hours, turning the pieces occasionally. Drain and reserve marinade.

Grill ducklings on a hot fire for about 40 minutes, basting continually with marinade and turning them frequently. Salt to taste shortly before they are done, then serve immediately.

Grilled Rock Cornish Hens

Yield: 4 servings

2 Rock Cornish hens
¾ cup wine vinegar
1 Tb crushed mixed herbs (e.g., sage, thyme, rosemary)
2 garlic cloves, cut in half
oil
salt and pepper

Cut birds in half, and clean the cavities. Wash well under cold running water and pat dry. Put birds in a deep dish, and marinate overnight in vinegar and water to cover, together with mixed herbs.

Drain the birds, pat dry, and rub well with cut side of garlic. Brush them lightly with oil, and grill over medium heat, basting occasionally with oil. Toward the end of the cooking period, when skin is crisp and golden brown, sprinkle with salt and pepper. Serve piping hot.

Grilled Squabs with Pepper Sauce

Yield: 4 servings

4 squab chickens (or Rock Cornish hens)
salt and pepper
melted butter
bread crumbs for dredging
1 lemon, cut in wedges
sweet pickles, sliced
Pepper Sauce (see Index).

Wash cleaned birds, and drain and dry well. Slit the back open, clean, and flatten slightly with a meat pounder or the flat side of a cleaver. Remove the smallest bones. Sprinkle the birds with salt and pepper, and brush with melted butter. Then dredge thoroughly in bread crumbs, and dribble on some more melted butter. Grill over a medium-hot fire for 20 to 30 minutes, until skin is nicely crisp and golden, basting frequently and turning the birds occasionally.

When fork-tender, transfer birds to a serving platter, and garnish with lemon wedges and sweet pickle slices. Accompany with Pepper Sauce, served separately in a sauceboat.

Bacon-Stuffed Squabs with Pepper Sauce

Yield: 4 servings

4 squab chickens
4 slices bacon
salt and pepper
oil
Pepper Sauce (see Index)

Clean and rinse birds well in cold water, reserving livers. Stuff each bird with 1 slice of bacon and 1 whole liver. Season inside and out with salt and pepper. Insert tips of leg bones in the cavity, and truss securely with fine cooking twine. Fasten the trussed birds on the spit, brush with a little oil, and grill over high heat for about 20 to 30 minutes, basting occasionally with oil and pan drippings. Serve with Pepper Sauce.

Savory Turkey on the Spit

Yield: 6 to 8 servings

1 small turkey (about 6–8 lb)
8 slices bacon
1 sprig sage
1 sprig rosemary
1 garlic clove
salt and pepper
2 Tb oil
juice of 1 lemon

Clean and rinse turkey, reserving giblets for other dishes. Mince half the bacon together with sage, rosemary, and garlic. Season with salt, and stuff this mixture inside turkey. Season outside lightly with salt and pepper, and brush with oil mixed with lemon juice. Wrap remaining 4 slices of bacon around turkey breast, and secure well with cooking twine.

Fasten turkey on the spit, and roast over medium heat for 2 to 2½ hours, depending on size. Baste occasionally with oil and lemon juice and pan drippings. Remove bacon strips just before turkey is done, and continue roasting until skin in nicely browned and very crisp. Let turkey stand for 15 minutes before carving.

Grilled Turkey Thighs

Yield: 4 servings

4 small turkey thighs
4 Tb butter, melted
salt and pepper

Brush turkey thighs with melted butter, season to taste with salt and pepper, and grill over medium heat for about 30 to 40 minutes, turning and basting the turkey pieces frequently. They are done when cooked to a crisp golden brown, and should be served piping hot. (A prepared sweet-and-sour barbecue sauce is a suitable accompaniment.)

Grilled Fish and Shellfish

Grilled Bass

Yield: 4 servings

1 freshwater or sea bass (about 3 to 3½ lb)
salt
2 Tb butter, melted
1 bunch parsley
6 Tb butter, softened
lemon juice

Clean fish, rinse thoroughly in cold water, and pat dry. Cut diagonal slashes in the sides, season with salt, and coat with melted butter. Cook on medium-hot grill, basting often and turning carefully only once.

Clean parsley and pat dry; reserve a few sprigs intact for garnish. Trim and chop remaining parsley. Cream softened butter in a bowl, then blend in chopped parsley and a few drops of lemon juice. Garnish grilled fish with parsley sprigs, and serve with parsley butter on the side.

Marinated Bass with Mustard Aioli

Yield: 4 to 6 servings

1 freshwater or sea bass (about 4–5 lb), cleaned
⅓ cup vinegar
3 Tb oil (preferably peanut or sesame)
sugar
1 tsp fennel seeds, crushed
5–6 sprigs fresh thyme, crushed (or rosemary; or ½ tsp dried)
salt and pepper
Mustard Aioli Sauce (see Index)

Rinse fish well in cold running water; drain well and pat dry. Slit open along midline, and fillet of large bones that can be easily removed. Prepare marinade with vinegar, oil, pinch of sugar, crushed fennel seeds and thyme, and salt and pepper. Set fish on a platter or in any large shallow dish, and pour marinade over it. Let stand for 1 hour or longer to absorb flavors. (Reserve marinade for later.)

Grill fish over a hot fire, for 10 to 12 minutes per side, turning only once and basting often with marinade. Serve accompanied with Mustard Aioli Sauce in a sauceboat.

Skewered Eel with Bay Leaf (p. 61)

Porgies Flambé (p. 65)

Bluefish with Garlic Sauce

Yield: 4 servings

4 small bluefish (about 1 lb each; or other slightly
  fatty, firm-fleshed fish such as mackerel)
oil
juice of 2 lemons
salt
black pepper, freshly ground
2 garlic cloves
2 black peppercorns
2 Tb chopped parsley
pinch of oregano
1 Tb vinegar

Clean the bluefish, wash them thoroughly in cold running water, pat dry, and cut several diagonal slashes in each. Set fish in a large deep dish. Combine ¼ cup oil, lemon juice, salt, and fresh ground pepper, then pour over the fish. Marinate for several hours, turning them occasionally.

Meanwhile, prepare a sauce by grinding garlic and peppercorns in a mortar, together with chopped parsley and oregano. To this seasoned paste, add several tablespoons of oil, according to taste, vinegar, and a little salt, blending well.

Drain and dry fish thoroughly, and grill on a hot fire, turning them occasionally and basting with marinade. When fish are nicely browned, serve with seasoned garlic sauce.

Dried Cod with Rosemary

Yield: 4 servings

2 lb dried salt cod
⅓ cup oil
juice of 2 lemons
salt and pepper
1 sprig rosemary, minced (or pinch of dried,
  crushed)

Soak the dried cod in cold water—for 8 to 10 hours if fish is somewhat flexible, for up to 24 hours hours if fish is very stiff and heavily salted. Change the soaking water every 6 to 8 hours. Cut the soaked cod in pieces about 3 inches square and pat dry. Mix thoroughly oil, lemon juice, and salt and pepper to taste. Pour this marinade over cod, then marinate for about 1 hour, turning the pieces of fish occasionally.

Oil a sheet of aluminum foil to cover the grill. Then, over glowing charcoal embers, set pieces of cod on the foil, pour remaining marinade over them, and sprinkle with rosemary. Cook, turning the pieces with a spatula occasionally, until fish can be flaked easily. (To ensure proper cooking and avoid burning the foil, cod should rest at least 4 inches above the coals.)

Grilled Smoked Cod

Yield: 4 servings

4 pieces smoked cod* (about ½ lb each)
oil
pepper
Maître d'Hôtel Butter (see Index)

Brush fish lightly with oil, sprinkle with a little pepper, and grill over medium heat for about 10 minutes. Turn two or three times, and baste occasionally during cooking.

Serve fish piping hot, accompanied with Maître d'Hôtel Butter in a sauceboat.

*Any lightly smoked, firm-fleshed fish is suitable for preparing this recipe.

Grilled Eel

Yield: 4 servings

2- to 2½-lb eel
salt and pepper
about 4 Tb oil
lemon juice
1 lemon, quartered
parsley sprigs

To prepare eel: Using a sharp-pointed knife, make an incision around the head of the eel. Using a kitchen towel to get a good grip, hold the fish tightly in one hand and, with a pair of pliers, skin with one swift tugging motion.

Clean under cold running water, pat dry, and cut in slices about 3 inches thick. Season with salt and pepper, rub with oil, sprinkle with some lemon juice, and let stand for about 10 minutes. Drain and cook on a medium-hot grill (preferably over a wood or charcoal fire) for about 15 minutes, turning slices several times.

Arrange slices of eel on a serving platter, and garnish with lemon wedges and parsley sprigs to serve.

Eels with Scallion and Butter Sauce

Yield: 4 servings

2 lb medium-size eels
oil
salt
1 cup dry red wine
2 Tb minced scallions
½ cup butter, softened
3 Tb chopped parsley

Skin eels as in preceding recipe fo Grilled Eel. Slit them lengthwise, clean and wash under cold running water, and remove backbone. Brush with oil and grill until tender, for about 10 minutes, turning them several times. Sprinkle with salt when half-done.

Just before eels are done, put wine and scallions in a saucepan, then simmer to reduce liquid to a few tablespoons. Remove from heat, and blend in butter and parsley. When eels are grilled to golden brown, serve them accompanied with sauce in a sauceboat.

Skewered Eel with Bay Leaf

Yield: 4 to 6 servings

1 medium-size eel (about 2 to 2½ lb)
⅓ cup oil
juice of 1 lemon
salt
black pepper, freshly ground
2 bay leaves, crushed
whole bay leaves
Tartar Sauce (see Index)

Prepare eel according to instructions for Grilled Eel. Combine oil, lemon juice, salt, plenty of fresh ground black pepper, and crushed bay leaves. Marinate eel in this mixture for about 1 hour, turning slices occasionally. Drain eel and pat dry, reserving marinade. Alternate eel slices with whole bay leaves on skewers. Grill for about 20 minutes on a medium-hot fire, basting occasionally with marinade.

This dish may be served with Tartar Sauce on the side. (Other suitable accompaniments are steamed fresh green beans and a garnish of lemon slices and parsley sprigs.)

61

Grilled Fillet of Flounder

Yield: 4 servings

2 to 2½ lb flounder fillets
¼ cup oil
¼ cup lemon juice
salt
black pepper, freshly ground
1 lemon, cut in wedges
Béarnaise Sauce (see Index)

Wash fish thoroughly in cold running water, and pat dry. Combine oil, lemon juice, and salt and pepper to taste. Place fillets on a platter, pour mixture over them, and marinate for about 1 hour.

Grill in a flat wire basket on a medium-hot fire, brushing fillets occasionally with marinade and turning them often to cook evenly on both sides. Garnish with lemon wedges, and accompany with Béarnaise Sauce in a sauceboat.

Fish and Vegetable Kabob

Yield: 4 servings

2 lb halibut steaks (or swordfish or other meaty fish steaks)
¼ cup lemon juice
¼ cup oil
2 Tb grated onion
2 Tb minced parsley
1 lb sweet peppers, cored and cut in strips
1 lb large fresh mushrooms (reserving stems for other use)
about 1 doz bay leaves
2 Tb butter, melted
1 lemon, quartered

Cut fish in 1½-inch cubes. Combine lemon juice, oil, onion, and parsley, and marinate fish cubes in this mixture for about 1 hour. Wash and trim vegetables.

Thread marinated fish on fine skewers, alternating pepper strips and mushroom caps and occasionally interspersing with a bay leaf. Set skewers on grill over medium-hot fire, and turn often to brown all sides, brushing frequently with remaining marinade and melted butter. Garnish with lemon wedges and additional chopped parsley, if desired.

Grilled Lobster Tails with French Sauce

Yield: 4 servings

4 large lobster tails (or 8 medium-size)
salt
4 Tb butter, melted
French Sauce (see Index)

If lobster tails are frozen, defrost slowly in main compartment of refrigerator. If tails are fresh rather than frozen (or when defrosted), with strong kitchen scissors, cut upper shell down the center, leaving the tail itself intact. Open cut shell out flat; remove digestive tract. Salt the lobster meat lightly, and set tails over a very hot fire, shell side down. Brush them with some melted butter, then grill for 15 to 20 minutes, or until tender and still juicy, turning them several times and basting occasionally with melted butter.

While lobster tails are cooking, prepare French Sauce to accompany them. When ready, arrange grilled lobster on a serving platter, pour on sauce generously, then either serve immediately or keep warm in a moderate oven or at the edge of the grill.

62

Lobster Tail Maria José (p. 64)

Lobster Tail Maria José

Yield: 4 servings

4 large lobster tails (or 8 medium-size)
1 stalk celery, chopped
1 small carrot, chopped
1 small onion, chopped
8 Tb butter
salt and pepper
pinch of tarragon
2 egg yolks
1 Tb heavy cream

Prepare lobster tails as in preceding recipe.

In a saucepan, sauté vegetables in 2 tablespoons of butter. When onion is wilted but not browned, season with salt and pepper and remove from heat. Melt 2 tablespoons of butter for basting lobster. Next, add tarragon and remaining 4 tablespoons of butter to vegetables in the pan. Cook over moderate heat. Beat egg yolks together with heavy cream, and add to the saucepan. As soon as sauce nears boiling point, remove from heat and strain through cheesecloth.

Preheat oven to 450°. Sprinkle lobster tails with salt and pepper, brush with a little melted butter, and put them over a very hot fire, shell side down. Grill for about 15 minutes, or until tender, turning and basting them occasionally. Transfer to a baking dish, cover with sauce, and pop into preheated oven for a few minutes to give a light, golden crust.

Grilled Mackerel

Yield: 4 servings

2 mackerel (about 1 to 1½ lb each)
¼ cup oil
salt and pepper
¼ cup chopped parsley
juice of 1 lemon
2 garlic cloves, sliced paper-thin
1 lemon, cut in wedges
parsley sprigs

Clean fish, wash thoroughly in cold running water, drain and pat dry, and set on a platter. Combine oil, salt, pepper, parsley, lemon juice, and thin-sliced garlic. Pour mixture over mackerel, and marinate for about 30 minutes, turning the fish occasionally.

Drain off and reserve marinade, dry fish well, and grill over high heat, turning them only once and basting frequently with marinade. When fish are nicely browned on the outside and flake easily, transfer to a serving platter and serve with lemon wedges and garnish of fresh parsley sprigs.